D0998717

RASHOMON

Rashomon

A PLAY BY
FAY & MICHAEL KANIN

Based on stories by
RYUNOSUKE AKUTAGAWA

RANDOM HOUSE · NEW YORK

To the Shining Memory of

JOEL

RASHOMON *was first presented by David Susskind and Hardy Smith at The Music Box, New York City, January 27, 1959, with the following cast:*

(IN ORDER OF APPEARANCE)

PRIEST	Michael Shillo
WOODCUTTER	Akim Tamiroff
WIGMAKER	Oscar Homolka
DEPUTY	Jack Bittner
BANDIT	Rod Steiger
HUSBAND	Noel Willman
WIFE	Claire Bloom
MOTHER	Ruth White
MEDIUM	Elsa Freed

Directed by Peter Glenville

Settings and costumes by Oliver Messel

Lighting by Jo Mielziner

Music by Laurence Rosenthal

Associate Producer, Michael Abbott

Produced by arrangement with Peter Cookson

The Scene

The action takes place in Kyoto,
Japan, about a thousand years
ago—at an edge of the Rashomon
Gate, at a Police Court, and
in a nearby forest.

The Setting

A single setting provides three separate locales.

At stage right, there is a suggestion of the Rashomon Gate. Before the time of our play, Rashomon was the largest gate in Kyoto, the ancient capital of Japan. It was 106 feet wide and 26 feet deep, its stone wall rising 75 feet and topped by a ridge pole. With the decline of West Kyoto, the Gate fell into bad repair and became a decayed relic with an unsavory reputation, a hideout for thieves and a dump for unclaimed corpses.

A small platform, projecting outward from the stage, serves to create the illusion of an ancient Police Court, from which the characters who testify face an unseen Magistrate, presumably in the position of the audience.

Commanding most of the stage is the forest outside of the city. Two separate parts of this forest will be seen at different times—one featuring a winding pathway, and the other a wide clearing within a grove of cedars and bamboo.

Each locale has its own distinct lighting. The Rashomon Gate is bleak, cold, rain-swept. The Police Court is shot through with a beam of bright sunlight. And in the forest the light filtering through the trees mottles everything with an intricate pattern of soft shadows.

ACT ONE

ACT ONE

Rashomon Gate.

The introductory music dissolves into the sound of the rain, as the lights come up on a section of this crumbling and deserted edifice which once served imposingly as the entrance to Kyoto. Now it huddles wet and gray and forlorn in the downpour, and seems more than ever removed from the mainstream of the living city. A large wooden dragon head, its crimson lacquer rubbed off badly, lies at the foot of the broken steps which are dotted with the white droppings of crows and with rank grass growing in the crevices.

The wind which signals the approaching dusk howls through the eaves of the Gate.

In a dry spot under the sagging roof, a Buddhist PRIEST *sits on the stone floor near a meager bonfire. Beside him is an improvised pack containing all his worldly belongings. His staff leans against a rotting post. He seems more tired than his thirty-odd years warrant—a study in defeat—as he holds his dark kimono about him and stares off into space.*

After a few moments, a WOODCUTTER *comes running through the rain toward the Gate. He wears a garment of homespun material, pulled up between his legs and held at his waist with a belt of rope. His handmade ax is stuck in his belt. He hurries*

3

up the steps of the Gate, looking around, then stops short as he sees the PRIEST. *He bows respectfully.*

WOODCUTTER (*Out of breath*) Forgive me, holy one—but—I've run all the way from the town. (*He indicates the direction from which he came*) I didn't believe them at the market place when they said, "The Priest has left us." I said, "You must be mistaken. He'll be back." (*He looks down at the significant pack beside the* PRIEST) Is it true, then? You *are* going away?
> (*The* PRIEST *nods slowly and his head sinks down into his hands desolately. The* WOODCUTTER *tries to speak but cannot find the words. He wipes the rain off his face helplessly. Then, suddenly, he can contain himself no longer*)

WOODCUTTER (*Bowing again*) I'm sorry—but I must speak. I know it was like a nightmare, something to make the flesh creep, what we saw and heard in the Police Court yesterday. It made no sense. (*Earnestly*) But to leave the Temple—your place here—that makes no sense either.

PRIEST What does make sense?

WOODCUTTER (*Shrugging*) I'm only a woodcutter. All I know is chopping wood till my muscles are numb and my hands look like horned toads.
> (*He looks at his hands ruefully*)

4

PRIEST (*Half to himself*) Earthquakes—

WOODCUTTER Huh?

PRIEST —fire, famine, pestilence—

WOODCUTTER These are natural things, like rain and sun. They're not supposed to make sense.

PRIEST And yet they do! An earthquake's violence I can understand. (*Rising*) But the savagery of men toward one another, and to themselves—
(*He crosses and stands looking off toward the road leading away from the city*)

WOODCUTTER There's no more shelter along that road. I know it well. (*Looking around*) This is a fearsome place—but it is better to wait here till the storm breaks.
(*The* PRIEST *turns back, his eyes wandering over their refuge. His hand moves over one of the rotting posts*)

PRIEST The great Rashomon Gate—(*A piece splinters off in his hand*) It crumbles—like the people.
(*From the direction of Kyoto, the Temple bells sound the hour*)

WOODCUTTER (*Looking off*) The Temple bells—they sound far away in the rain. (*Embarrassedly*) I myself seldom go to

5

the Temple. My clothes always smelling of rotting wood. (*Then*) But I've heard them speak of you. They say you've taught the people much.

PRIEST (*Bitterly*) You were with me at the Court yesterday. You saw how well they learned.

WOODCUTTER I can't understand it. Such horrible crimes—rape, bloodshed. And then, in front of the Magistrate to make it all —worse— (*Shaking his head*) There must be an answer, but I'm too ignorant to know what it is.

PRIEST No more ignorant than I.

WOODCUTTER That's not so! You're a holy man—a wise man—

PRIEST (*With rising emotion*) Am I? Then why do those faces burn in my mind just as in yours—and those monstrous words echo in my ears, calling for answers I cannot give? (*There is a distant roll of thunder. The* WOODCUTTER *looks upward, uneasily*) The all-seeing Buddha knows—he knows how unworthy I am.
  (*He sinks down beside the bonfire again*)

WOODCUTTER Please—don't say that.

PRIEST My father was a rich mirror-maker in Kiwa. He didn't want me to be a priest, but *I* wanted it. A man doesn't look

6

for his soul in a mirror, I told him. (*He turns away wearily*)
Perhaps my father was right.

(*The* WOODCUTTER *stares at him, at a loss*)

WOODCUTTER Where will you go?

PRIEST I don't know—I don't know—

WIGMAKER'S VOICE (*From above*) Why don't you go to one of
the eight fiery hells? (*The suddenness of the voice startles a
few crows and they caw complainingly. The* PRIEST *and*
WOODCUTTER, *startled too, look up as the* WIGMAKER'S *head
appears among the rafters above, muttering*) Can't find a
place to sleep in peace any more—

(*He starts to climb down with remarkable assurance for
his sixty-odd years. He wears a faded and torn garment
with a catch-all bag slung over his shoulder. His face is
a mass of wrinkles and his body gnarled, but there is
about him the alertness and resourcefulness of one who
has learned to live in the jungle. It's hard to believe that
he was ever, even at birth, anything but a cynic*)

WOODCUTTER (*Turning to the* PRIEST *apprehensively*) Let's go
to another part of the Gate, holy one.

PRIEST Why?

WOODCUTTER Please—you never know what you'll encounter
here.

7

WIGMAKER (*Coming down*)   Caw—caw—caw!

WOODCUTTER (*Turning on him*)   Hold your tongue, you scavenger!

WIGMAKER (*As he drops to the ground*)   Hold *my* tongue? What about *your* tongue—and the hairless one's?

WOODCUTTER (*Angrily*)   Don't be so low! This is a *priest* you're talking to.

WIGMAKER   Impossible. He woke me up. They usually put me to sleep.

WOODCUTTER (*To the* PRIEST, *protectively*)   Please don't listen—

PRIEST   Who is he?

WOODCUTTER   He's a thief, a jackal—an old swindler!

WIGMAKER   How else can you live to be old nowadays? (*To the* PRIEST, *with a mock-formal bow*)   If you want to know—I'm a wigmaker.

WOODCUTTER   Wigmaker! With hair stolen from corpses!

8

WIGMAKER   The very finest corpses in Kyoto. Interred by their loved ones in the dung heaps of the Rashomon Gate. The crows and I administer the last rites. (*To the* PRIEST) Now that you're giving up the priesthood, maybe I can make a wig for you—a long, fancy one. (*The* PRIEST *rises and moves away, and the* WIGMAKER *shakes his head, grinning*) Excuse me—I'm not used to such tender sensibilities around here. My friends, the corpses, never take offense at anything. (*Rubbing himself as if chilly, he proceeds to gather some stray pieces of wood and to toss them on the bonfire*) There's one, for instance, a female—beautiful black hair—used to sell dried snake meat to the soldiers. Told them it was fish. She'd still be doing it, if the plague hadn't gotten her. I'm sure *she'd* understand. (*Squatting down beside the fire*) Oh, you'd like them all now. They've given up gossip, cursing, stealing, fighting. Sure, they stink a little, but no more than some live ones I know.

(*The* WOODCUTTER *glares at him, then turns to the* PRIEST)

WOODCUTTER   He's as bad as the three at the Police Court yesterday.

WIGMAKER (*Over his shoulder*)   As bad as I am? Now, that interests me. Who were they? (*As they are silent*) What happened?

WOODCUTTER (*After a pause, grudgingly*)   A man was murdered.

9

WIGMAKER   Just one? A slow day.

> (*After a moment, the* WOODCUTTER *shuffles over and kneels down beside the fire, too, warming his hands as the* WIGMAKER *fans the feeble flames*)

WOODCUTTER   It wasn't the murder alone. It was—how it happened, the things we heard at the Police Court—

WIGMAKER *(Indicating the* PRIEST)   He was there, too?

WOODCUTTER   We were called, both of us, to testify.

WIGMAKER   Why?

WOODCUTTER   It was I who found the body.

WIGMAKER *(Impressed)*   Where?

WOODCUTTER   In the woods. East of the city. It was late in the afternoon, at the hour of the ox. It's too hot these days, even in the forest, to cut wood in the middle of the day. So I wait until—

WIGMAKER *(Impatiently)*   And you came upon this body?

WOODCUTTER   No. I mean, not at first. First, I saw the sedge hat, with a veil on it, dangling from a bush—

WIGMAKER A woman's?

WOODCUTTER Yes. It looked odd hanging there—women don't come into the forest very often. I called, but there was no answer. So I went on. And a few steps farther I saw a tortoise-shell comb on the path—and then a piece of rope. And then—

(*He stops*)

WIGMAKER (*Eagerly*) Yes?

WOODCUTTER And then—an arm. Just an arm, sticking out from a clump of bamboo shoots—the fingers all stiff and twisted. For a moment I thought it was some strange plant. Then, in the shadows behind it I saw the face, eyes empty and staring, the mouth gaping—

WIGMAKER I know, they always look surprised. Death must be a lot different than anyone imagines.

WOODCUTTER I ran—the brush tore at my legs and arms till they bled. But I didn't stop till I reached the Police and told them. (*Mopping his face*) And then, yesterday, they asked us to appear.

WIGMAKER (*Remembering the* PRIEST) But—what did *he* have to do with it?

WOODCUTTER He *saw* them both, on their way—before they entered the forest.

WIGMAKER Both? (*Turning to the* PRIEST) Then there *was* a woman?

PRIEST (*Nodding*) Yes. The murdered man's wife. I passed them on the road from Sekiyama, in the early afternoon. She was seated on a horse, he was leading it. He looked so formidable in his samurai robes—his sword at his side, a bow and quiver on his back. He looked so—(*With a sigh*)—so alive.

WIGMAKER How was he killed?

WOODCUTTER Run through—with a sword.

PRIEST But no weapon was found.

WIGMAKER (*To the* WOODCUTTER) And you saw none?

WOODCUTTER What? No, no—the hand, the face, was all I saw and all I wanted to see. I ran out of there fast!

WIGMAKER Everyone's always running away from the dead. What can a corpse do? Take my advice—run from the *live* ones. (*Throws a few more sticks on the fire*) Any idea who did the sticking?

WOODCUTTER They arrested someone.

WIGMAKER They always arrest someone. But is he guilty?

WOODCUTTER It's Tajomaru.

WIGMAKER (*Eyes widening*) Tajomaru! Then for once they've gotten the right man.

PRIEST I'm not sure.

WIGMAKER (*Rising incredulously*) The most dangerous bandit in this part of the country and you're not sure? If he were within twenty miles of any crime, I'd convict him of it!

PRIEST It's not quite so simple—

WIGMAKER (*Mimicking his tone*) Not quite so simple. (*With growing anger*) If it were *me* they caught, it would be simple enough! Steal a coin, a pair of sandals, a chicken so scrawny you can't get your teeth into it—pull a hair from the head of some poor cadaver who has no more use for it—and you're a sneak thief, lower than a viper. But rob someone of a fortune —kill, rape, plunder, loot in a *big* way—and soon you're a figure of a man with a magic name. Soon they're talking about you, telling stories and singing songs about you. Soon you're someone to be reckoned with—and "it's not quite so simple!"

(*He spits on the ground disgustedly*)

PRIEST   You weren't there—you don't know the things he said.

WIGMAKER   Well, what *did* he say—Tajomaru? (*Quickly*) Not that I'd believe a word of it.

WOODCUTTER (*To the* PRIEST)   He sounds just like the Deputy. Do you remember what he said in the Police Court?

WIGMAKER (*Sitting*)   Deputy? What deputy?

WOODCUTTER   The one who captured Tajomaru. He used almost the same words when he talked to the Magistrate. "Your Excellency," he said, "this is Tajomaru, the killer, the rapist, the plunderer, the terror of our roads and forests. As proof of his guilt—I submit—"

(*As the* WOODCUTTER *speaks, the voice of the* DEPUTY *gradually takes over. At the same time, the lights on the Rashomon Gate slowly dim out as others come up on the Police Court. The* DEPUTY, *a small but wiry man, is kneeling on a grass mat facing the unseen* MAGISTRATE— *who is in the position of the audience—and holding a scroll opened to a considerable length. Next to him, the bandit,* TAJOMARU, *sits indolently gazing upward, his wrists bound behind him. He wears a rough, loose robe of the period, his chest partly bared*)

DEPUTY (*Continuing the* WOODCUTTER's *speech*) —I submit to you his record, a list of the crimes absolutely known to have been committed by him. Unfortunately, there was not sufficient time to complete it. (*He bows*) Thank you, Your Excellency. (*Rolling up the scroll*) It was in the early hours of night on the river beach of Katsura. I came upon him groaning on the sand. He must have been thrown by the horse that was standing a few yards away. (*As* TAJOMARU *snorts without looking at him*) . . . A white horse, Your Excellency, with a fine mane. It matches the description of the one owned by the murdered man. Also, a bow wound with leather strips, a black lacquered quiver and seventeen arrows with hawk feathers—they were next to him. . . . Wearing? (*With a glance at* TAJOMARU) The same as now. Also a large plain sword. . . . No, there was no sign of a woman around. He was alone and in great agony. (*Smirking*) It must be more painful to be thrown from a stolen horse than from any other. (*As* TAJOMARU *laughs derisively, the* DEPUTY *stops, then continues hesitantly*) As I said, I went over to where he had fallen, and—

TAJOMARU Tajomaru fall from a horse? (*He spits at the* DEPUTY, *who retreats a little*) There's no horse living can throw Tajomaru! I was sick—poisoned! (*Contemptuously*) He captured me! (*With one foot, he kicks at the* DEPUTY, *who recoils*) Go away, little bug, before I step on you!

DEPUTY (*To the* MAGISTRATE, *protestingly*) Your Excellency—

TAJOMARU (*To the* MAGISTRATE) Do we have to listen all day to this puffing about what a great hero he is? You want to know what happened? I'll tell it myself.

DEPUTY But I just—(*As the* MAGISTRATE *obviously dismisses him, he bows deeply*) . . . Yes, Your Excellency. As you wish.
(*Still bowing, he backs off into the darkness and disappears*)

TAJOMARU Tajomaru thrown from a horse— Hah! He was a good horse, that one, strong and sure-footed. I ran him hard all day. But it was hot—I got thirsty. Near the Osaka Pass is a stream—you may know it—the water comes down sweet from the mountains. But it wasn't sweet this day. Something must have poisoned it—a dead serpent, maybe, in the upper stream. I rode on an hour or so and then my belly began to swell. I got dizzy. I don't feel pain like other men, but this— (*His face contorts*) Near the river bed I couldn't bear it any longer. I got off the horse and doubled over on the ground and—(*He stops, doubled over, remembering the agony. Then he shakes off the weak moment*) Tajomaru fall off a horse! Only a fool could have such a foolish idea. (*As the* MAGISTRATE *directs a question to him*) . . . The man? Did I kill him? (*He shrugs*) I know I'll hang from a tree on the execution ground no matter what I say. I can see you've decided the time has come for me to pay for my crimes—the ones I've done, the ones you think I've done and the ones you're afraid I might do. So why should I lie? (*Breaking his bonds in a gesture of strength and defiance*) Yes, it was I,

Tajomaru, who killed the man! . . . Why? (*He smiles*)
Because of a little breeze. (*Nodding*) . . . You heard it right.
A little breeze that swept through the green leaves. If it
hadn't been for that, the man would never have been killed.
(*He rises, as the lights start slowly to dim on the Police
Court and come up on the winding pathway in the forest*)
It was during the deadly heat of the afternoon. When it's so
hot, a man's jaws stretch, his legs grow heavy— (*He yawns,
moving lazily out of the Court, toward the forest*) And when
your legs grow heavy—(*He stretches*)—there's only one
thing—to do—

(*The lights are out on the Court now and up full on the
forest.* TAJOMARU *drops down on a grassy knoll. Stretch-
ing out, he scratches himself luxuriously, closing his eyes.
There is a long, quiet pause. Then, from the depths
of the forest, the* HUSBAND *and* WIFE *appear. The*
HUSBAND *is dressed in the robe of a samurai warrior;
he wears a sword with an elaborate silver handle and
has a quiver of arrows across his back. His hands,
the shape of his head, and his bearing show breed-
ing and position as contrasted with the gross animal
virility of the bandit. He leads a small white horse on
which his* WIFE *is riding. The* WIFE *is dressed in a kimono
of brilliant hue, rich but suitable for traveling. She wears
a large sedge hat, from which is draped a long veil, not
unlike a mosquito netting, that completely obscures her
face. The* HUSBAND, *noticing* TAJOMARU, *stops suspiciously.*
TAJOMARU *opens his eyes drowsily for a moment, then
closes them again. The* HUSBAND *continues, leading the*

17

horse. As they get closer to TAJOMARU, *a breeze flutters through the leaves, blowing the woman's veil.* TAJOMARU'S *eyes open sleepily at the moment that the rippling veil allows a glimpse of her face. His eyes remain open as the pair continues across the stage. He lies there for a second, tensely now, then sits up, turning his head to look after them. As they are about to exit, he jumps up abruptly, simultaneously picking up his sword, which was lying by his side*)

TAJOMARU Ey! (*The* HUSBAND *wheels, holding the bridle of the horse. He looks at* TAJOMARU, *then slowly leads the horse back toward him and stops.* TAJOMARU *looks up at the woman, back at the man. Then he walks deliberately around the horse, examining the man and woman from all sides. The* HUSBAND'S *hand goes slowly toward his sword.* TAJOMARU *notices the* HUSBAND'S *action*) That's a fancy sword. (*The* HUSBAND'S *hand rests on it*) Silver handle? (*The* HUSBAND *doesn't answer.* TAJOMARU *laughs reassuringly, sticking his own sword in his belt*) Thirsty? (*The* HUSBAND *watches him, noncommittal.* TAJOMARU *takes a water pouch from his belt, holds it out in a friendly gesture. The* HUSBAND *does not move.* TAJOMARU *grins and takes a swallow himself to show that the water is not poisoned*) You have no water pouches and it's two miles to the next stream. (*The* HUSBAND *wets his dry lips with his tongue, weighing the offer. Then he takes the water pouch, offers it to the woman. She shakes her head. The* HUSBAND *lifts the pouch to his lips and drinks deeply, then tosses the pouch back to* TAJOMARU) Going to Kyoto?

HUSBAND Passing through.
> (*He puts his hand on the horse's bridle as if to start again*)

TAJOMARU You like swords? (*The* HUSBAND *looks at him*) Silver handles like yours—gold handles—stones in them, red, green? (*The* HUSBAND *tries to mask his interest*) There's an ancient tomb in the mountain. I came across it—dug it open. It was full of things like that. (*Shrugging*) They're no good to me. If you're interested, I'll sell you some, cheap.

HUSBAND (*After a long moment*) Gold handles?

TAJOMARU With stones. Red, green—
> (*There is a moment, then the* HUSBAND *shakes his head*)

HUSBAND No.
> (*He turns to go, shifting his hand on the horse's bridle*)

TAJOMARU (*As though unconcerned*) All right—I'll sell them to someone else.
> (*He starts away. The* HUSBAND *looks after* TAJOMARU, *temptation fighting it out against caution*)

HUSBAND (*Abruptly*) Where are they?

TAJOMARU (*Turning quickly*) Over there, in that next grove. (*Crossing and pointing off*) See—beyond the bamboos, where the cedars are.
> (*The* HUSBAND'S *eyes follow the pointing finger. He studies* TAJOMARU *narrowly*)

HUSBAND (*Finally making the decision*)   Wait.
    (*He leads the horse into the woods, tying the rein to the
    branch of a tree. Then he comes back to* TAJOMARU, *who
    makes an obsequious gesture, as if to say, "After* you."
    The HUSBAND *turns and goes off through the trees.*
    TAJOMARU *starts to follow, then slows up and stops, look-
    ing after him. He turns back, as the lights slowly start to
    dim on the forest*)

TAJOMARU   As I said—a little puff of air. And I saw a woman's
    face. Or was it a vision? (*He moves into the Police Court,
    on which the lights are coming up*) I had to know. In that
    first moment, I made up my mind to take her. Even if I had
    to kill the man. (*He squats down, facing the* MAGISTRATE)
    To me, killing isn't a matter of great importance. Blood is
    ugly to you "polite" people who kill with power and money
    instead of the sword. Sometimes you even say it's for their
    own good, the ones you destroy. They don't squirm or cry
    or bleed—they're in the best of health. But all the same—(*He
    stops at the* MAGISTRATE's *obvious reprimand*) . . . I *am*
    giving you the facts. Didn't I say I killed the man? You
    asked me why. I kill to live, to eat, to have pleasure. When-
    ever I capture a woman, I always have to kill her man. But
    this time, it's funny—this time I didn't mean to kill him. I
    thought if I could take a woman once without killing the
    man, it would be—(*There is a pause. Then he shrugs, un-
    able to explain it*) So I made my plans to get him out of the
    way and have the woman alone. It was easy. He was greedy,
    like all of them are. He went with me to the bamboo grove.

When we got there, I seized him from behind. He was a trained warrior and strong—I had to take him by surprise. He struggled like a trapped tiger. But I tied him up to the root of a bamboo. (*He shakes his head ruefully at the memory of the struggle*) Then I thought of the woman—(*The lights start to come up on the forest*)—all alone there, waiting for him. (*He rises, starts backing toward the forest*) And I went back to her.

(*The lights dim quickly on the Police Court as the forest lighting comes up full.* TAJOMARU *turns, runs stealthily into the woods and crouches behind a bush. The* WIFE *has dismounted from the horse and is walking among the trees, her veil still concealing her face. She is having a flirtation with an unseen bird. The bird chirps. The woman answers him, echoing his chirp, seating herself in the coolness of the grassy knoll. Silently,* TAJOMARU *moves to a closer bush, watching her intently from behind the masking leaves. The bird speaks again—the woman answers. As the bird replies, the woman laughs —a bit of delicate music in her throat. Suddenly, as if somehow aware of the eyes on her, she wheels toward the bush.* TAJOMARU, *caught, rises and emerges awkwardly*)

TAJOMARU Your husband—he says to wait here. He—he's picking out what he wants—(*The woman rises and faces him, silently, as he comes closer*) There are many things for him to look at. Swords and—mirrors. It—it will take him—(*Abruptly, she lifts the veil and stares up at him. He stops at*

the full sight of her face—delicate, exquisite—his words trickling off)—some—time—
(There is a long silence as they look at each other)

WIFE   What have you done with him?
(TAJOMARU doesn't answer. Her eyes search his desperately for a long moment. Then suddenly she runs past him—off in the direction in which her husband disappeared. TAJOMARU stands looking after her)

TAJOMARU   I could have stopped her—(*The lighting changes as he moves toward the Police Court, still looking after her*) But that look on her face—the eyes wide and startled, like a deer, the lips trembling—(*Facing the* MAGISTRATE) It made me jealous—jealous that he could make her look like that. Suddenly, I wanted her to see the ugly sight of him tied to the tree—weak, helpless, looking like a fool—(*Shaking his head*) I can't understand it, even now. Anyway—(*The lights are slowly coming up on the forest*) I let her go to him. And I followed—
(He turns and disappears into the forest. The stage revolves to show us the clearing in the bamboo grove. His hands tied behind him, the HUSBAND *is secured to a bamboo stump, straining ineffectually against his bonds. There is a rustling in the thicket and the* WIFE *appears, her sedge hat lost en route. Searching in and out among the trees, she finally stops short at the sight of her* HUSBAND. *They stare at each other—she, horrified; his face pale with shame at her witnessing his plight.* TAJOMARU*

Rod Steiger, Claire Bloom, and Noel Willman,
as TAJOMARU, the WIFE, and the HUSBAND

appears, coming up behind the WIFE. *He stands watching
them with an arrogant smile, enjoying the success of his
plan. The woman slowly turns to look at him, then back
at her* HUSBAND *as the significance of what this means
begins to flood over her. Suddenly, she pulls a dagger
concealed in her robe and leaps at* TAJOMARU. *He eludes
her and she chases him, lashing out wildly with the
dagger. Such a show of spirit and temper is more than*
TAJOMARU *counted on. He begins to grow more excited
as he laughs, leading her on, always managing to escape
from her furious thrusts. Panting now, her hair loosened,
her face flushed, the woman fights on, almost hysterical
with anger and frustration. The* HUSBAND *strains in vain
against his bonds. Suddenly catching the woman's wrist,*
TAJOMARU *bends it until, with a cry, she drops the dagger.
Then, holding her writhing body, his mouth seeks hers,
his arms bending her to his embrace. The* HUSBAND *closes
his eyes, turning his head away from the sight. Under*
TAJOMARU'S *lips, the woman struggles wildly, then gradually the struggle grows less. And then, after a long moment, her hand moves subtly along* TAJOMARU'S *back to
clasp him in a return embrace. There is suddenly the
sound of the* WIGMAKER'S *raucous laugh from the darkness. The lights fade out and simultaneously fade in on
the Rashomon Gate*)

WIGMAKER (*Enjoying it vicariously*) That's Tajomaru, all
right! No mistake. Even among bandits, he's famous for his
lechery. (*Moving closer to the other two*) Just two months

ago, in the mountain pass behind the Toribe Temple, a lady of the court was waylaid, with her mother and her daughter. Three pieces of fruit from the same tree. Which one do you think Tajomaru picked? (*Looking at them expectantly, as they're silent*) The lady? The daughter? The mother? (*He laughs boisterously*) All three of them!

WOODCUTTER (*Outraged*)   Tajomaru's a savage—a wild beast!

WIGMAKER   But the women seem to like it. Especially the high-born ones with their airs and downcast eyes. Show them a man with sweat on him and their tongues grow big in their mouths.

(*He illustrates his point vulgarly. The* PRIEST *rises and crosses away*)

WOODCUTTER (*Angrily*)   Have you no respect? To talk so before a Priest!

WIGMAKER   He said he's giving it up. (*With a shrug*) If he's going to join the rest of us, he may as well start learning the language. (*The* WOODCUTTER *gets up, too, and moves away, watching the* PRIEST) All right, tell me more. Your story warms me more than this sickly fire. (*With a grimace, he blows on it, fanning up the flames a trifle*) What else did he say—Tajomaru?

WOODCUTTER   Nothing!

WIGMAKER   Nothing? I don't believe it. Half the pleasure of taking a woman is talking about it afterwards. (*Appeasingly*) Come on, he must've said *something* more. (*To the* PRIEST) Didn't he?

PRIEST (*Slowly*)   Yes, he said—more. He said—he never meant to kill.

> (*The lights fade out on the Gate and come up on the Court—as* TAJOMARU *appears out of the darkness to face the* MAGISTRATE *again*)

TAJOMARU   That's the way I planned it—without killing. ... That's right, without killing the husband. All I wanted was the woman. (*He stops, remembering*) I've had many women. When you think about it later, there's not much difference in them. Some fight you, some don't. But this one—(*Puzzled*) I don't know—I was sure her body was eager, her mouth hot under mine. And yet, when I stood up from her, she just lay there—crying—

> (*The lights have changed to the forest. The* WIFE *is lying on the ground, crying softly. The* HUSBAND *sits, his eyes tightly shut, his face taut with anger and humiliation.* TAJOMARU *strides into the scene. He paces past the woman, stops, looks at her impatiently, paces back again, turns, then crosses to her*)

TAJOMARU   Oh, stop that! (*He walks away, then turns back*) I didn't hurt you—you're not going to die! (*After a moment, as she keeps on crying softly*) Stop it, I tell you! There's your husband—untie him and go on your way.

(*With a gesture of dismissal, he turns and starts to exit off through the woods. The* WIFE *sits up and turns toward him*)

WIFE   Wait—please—

TAJOMARU (*Stops and turns*)   What do you want?

WIFE   How can I live—disgraced in the eyes of two men?

TAJOMARU (*Looks at her narrowly*)   What does it matter what *I* think of you? You'll never see me again.

WIFE   I'll always see you. (*Closing her eyes to shut out the horror of it*) Awake or asleep—this grove, this tree, this piece of ground—I'll see it all till I die. (*As the bandit smiles, not displeased with the thought, she turns her tear-filled eyes toward him*) At least, give my husband a chance to avenge my honor—and his own.

TAJOMARU   Why should I?

WIFE   I beg you.

TAJOMARU   This is no place to worry about honor.

26

WIFE (*With great difficulty*) Give him a chance. If he fails, I'll—go with you—be your woman. (TAJOMARU *stands, evaluating her. Her eyes lower under his gaze*) Even a bandit must have *some* feeling—*some* sense of justice.

TAJOMARU Justice? (*He snorts at the crudity of this trap*) He's a samurai, trained in the art of fighting. Do you think I'm a fool to let you trap me with pretty words—so that he can kill me? (*As she watches him, her lips tremulous*) Or could I be wrong? Are you hoping, maybe, that I'll kill *him?* Would that be more to your liking? (*Provocatively*) There are always women. Why should I take a chance for *you?*
  (*For a long moment, her desperate eyes search his. Then, abruptly, she crawls over and picks up her dagger lying on the ground near them. As her* HUSBAND *struggles vainly against his bonds, she raises the dagger to plunge it into her throat. But* TAJOMARU *springs forward, wrenches it from her hand and tosses it away. With an exultant laugh, he grasps her by the hair and kisses her roughly. Then, pushing her away, he crosses to the* HUSBAND, *draws his sword and cuts the* HUSBAND's *bonds —at the same time leaping back, sword raised. The* HUSBAND *springs to his feet and draws his own sword. And he attacks with a ferocity demanded by his pent-up anger and emotion, raining violent blows at* TAJOMARU, *as though to chop him to bits in the first charge. But the bandit defends himself well. His technique, obviously self-taught, is not as classically formal as the* HUSBAND's. *But it is just as effective, springing as it does out of daily*

27

use in the cause of primitive self-preservation. It isn't long before the HUSBAND *realizes that, against such an opponent, he cannot afford to exhaust himself in emotion and useless swordplay. All over the grove, they attack and defend, each in turn—tensely, grimly—both aware that they are fighting to the death. The* WIFE, *watching this fateful struggle, shrinks farther and farther into the shadows behind her. Finally, after an intricate exchange, the* HUSBAND *strikes a well-timed blow that sends* TAJO-MARU'S *sword flying from his hands. Following up this advantage, he aims a head cut at the bandit, who, flinging himself away from the blow, falls flat on his back. With a triumphant shout, the* HUSBAND *extends his sword toward the bandit's throat. In that long moment before death, the point of the sword moves closer and closer to* TAJOMARU'S *throat. Even facing the cold steel, the bandit glares up at the* HUSBAND *arrogantly and not without a touch of admiration. Abruptly, he tries to slither away on his back, but the* HUSBAND *is close on him, the sword point never leaving his throat. As the bandit's muscles seem to go limp in apparent resignation, the* HUSBAND *takes a solid stance and raises the sword for the finishing blow. But* TAJOMARU, *with animal-like cunning, swiftly grabs both of the* HUSBAND'S *legs and slams him to the ground. The sword flies from the* HUSBAND'S *grasp. There is a wildly desperate scramble, accompanied by grunts and shouts, as each tries to reach the weapon and prevent the other from doing so.* TAJOMARU *gets to his feet, is tripped by the* HUSBAND, *who crawls for the sword.*

But the bandit recovers in time to run over and shove the HUSBAND *into a clump of bamboo just as he's reaching for the sword. Panting,* TAJOMARU *picks up the weapon himself, raises it high over his head and plunges it down to its fatal conclusion. There is a chilling cry and a gasp from the bamboo clump. Then silence.* TAJOMARU *straightens slowly, struggling for breath, and stands for a moment looking down at the dead man. Then, coming back to the center of the clearing, he looks around for the* WIFE, *but she is nowhere in sight. He turns slowly and starts toward the Court)*

TAJOMARU He fought very well. *(The lights fade out on the forest and come up on the Police Court as* TAJOMARU *steps into it, facing the* MAGISTRATE) Too well. Trained warriors should fight other trained warriors. In the jungle, they haven't got a chance. *(Appreciatively)* Still, he was the only man who ever crossed swords with Tajomaru more than fifteen times. . . . The woman? *(He shrugs, sitting on the floor indifferently)* How do I know? She must have run away—she was nowhere around. I found her horse still grazing on the path, so I took it. And I sold her dagger for drinks. *Lots* of drinks—it had a mother-of-pearl handle. *(He laughs ironically. Then, at a question from the* MAGISTRATE, *he shakes his head)* . . . No, I didn't look for her. It must have been her temper that attracted me. But she was—just a woman, after all.

(The lights darken on the Police Court and come up on the Rashomon Gate. The three men are huddled around the fire)

29

WIGMAKER   He didn't look for her—(*He snorts*) No wonder. One of these days they'll find her, face down, in a gully.

WOODCUTTER   What do you mean?

WIGMAKER   What's another killing to a man like Tajomaru?

PRIEST   No, he didn't kill her.

WOODCUTTER   The woman appeared at the Police Court.

WIGMAKER (*Stops laughing*)   She appeared?

WOODCUTTER   The police found her—near a shrine, not far away. She was hiding there.

WIGMAKER   Well, she won't have to hide any more. With Tajomaru's confession and with her there to accuse him, he'll hang before morning.
   (*There is an oddly human cawing sound*)

WOODCUTTER (*Startled*)   What's that noise?

WIGMAKER (*Looking upward*)   The crows. They love to hear about hangings.
   (*He laughs*)

PRIEST   But the wife—she *didn't* accuse him. She told a completely different story.

WIGMAKER Different? How could it be different? Tajomaru confessed, didn't he?

PRIEST It's odd, but I found her not at all as Tajomaru described her. Nothing of worldliness, of vanity—of temper. Watching her there, I saw a face so delicate and defenseless— the eyes, like those of a bird with a broken wing you hold in your hand—

> (*As he describes the* WIFE, *a spotlight fades in, pinpointing her face. Slowly, the lights fade out on the Rashomon Gate and come up fully on the Police Court. The* WIFE *is sitting on the mat, staring emptily. Kneeling beside her is an elderly woman who is bowing to the* MAGISTRATE)

MOTHER . . . Yes, Your Excellency. This is my daughter, Kinume—my only daughter—my poor child who stares at me with vacant eyes—(*Nodding resignedly*) I can see it in your face—you're surprised to see a beautiful lotus risen from such a muddy pond. The Goddess of Fertility was good to me. Seven years I prayed to her, seven childless years. And in the eighth year, in the month of the cherry flowers— Kinume was born. Like a cherry flower herself, tiny and delicate and fragrant in my arms. (*Proudly*) And I always kept her so. Not like the other children in their commonplace robes, but in a long-sleeved, many-colored dress of rare silk, her hair caught up with a tortoise comb. Each morning she went to the writing school—never stumbling or dirtying her dainty hands—carrying her copybooks with such grace

31

all eyes turned to watch—(*Brought back abruptly by the* MAGISTRATE, *she bows*) . . . Forgive me, Your Excellency. But, seeing my daughter again, I—(*She nods*) . . . Yes, it is so. The dead man I looked upon was her husband. His name was Takehiko. He was a samurai in the town of Kofu—a very noble man, very rich. In the funeral procession, I will carry a cage of birds and set them free to remind everyone of his mercy and kindness. I'm sure he did nothing to bring such a horrible death on himself. (*Shaking her head*) Horrible! I hope you'll bring the villain who murdered him to justice. These bandits who roam our lands and prey upon us like wild beasts—they should be *dealt* with like wild beasts! (*Listening*) . . . *When,* Your Excellency? Four years ago they were married. It was a big wedding—the joining of two fine families. (*Confidently*) You have only to look at her to understand that my daughter was much sought-after. She had many offers, all of very high rank. But Takehiko was the most eager—and the most worthy. Even so, she was very proud—I had to *persuade* her to marry him—

WIFE (*Abruptly*) Have you no shame? (*The* MOTHER *turns, startled, to face her daughter's tortured eyes*) To stand in the presence of death—and still have vanity?

MOTHER (*Turning nervously to the* MAGISTRATE) You must excuse her, Your Excellency. Her mind is still unclear—the shock of her ordeal—

WIFE (*To the* MAGISTRATE) My husband *was* a samurai in

32

Kofu. And my mother was a maidservant in his house.
(*There is a moment, then the* MOTHER *lowers her head*)

MOTHER (*Brokenly*) What does it matter if it pleases me to
tickle myself with small fancies? It hurts no one.

WIFE It is no time for fancies—even small ones. (*Turning to
the* MAGISTRATE) She was a good and trusted servant. That's
also something to be proud of. Very often I helped her—drew
the water from the well and stirred it round with pine leaves,
brought it in a crystal bowl for his bedchamber. From the
time I was a child, I learned to follow the gold threads in his
robe with my needle. And with my eyes I watched him—and
loved him—never thinking, never daring to think it was pos-
sible. It seemed he never looked at me, except as you look at
a window and see past it. And then, one day—(*Her face
reflects the memory*) I wore a flower in my hair—a red peony.
He reached out his hand and touched it. I remember how my
cheeks burned and my mouth grew dry—(*Fighting back the
rush of tears*) I tried to be the wife he wanted—a samurai's
wife. The clothes I wore, he chose. I learned to walk, to talk,
to hold the rice bowl as he wished. I lay at his side at night
afraid to sleep so that I shouldn't waken and find it all a
dream. (*Her lips tremble*) A dream—(*She puts her hands
to her face, sobbing. Finally, as if by the urging of the* MAGIS-
TRATE, *she gains control of herself*) . . . I know, Your Excellency. And I'll try to talk calmly. I'll try to remember it all
—as it happened. (*She continues, strainedly*) When the

33

bandit had—finished with me, he strutted about like a pea-
cock, describing his many conquests, comparing me to the
others in low, vile language. (*Shaking her head*) For my
husband, how terrible it must have been—bound, helpless.
Even now, I can still hear the bandit's laughter—(*She pulls
herself to her feet, her hands going to her ears to shut out
the sound as* TAJOMARU's *laughter is heard from the darkness.
She moves backward toward the clearing, as the lights change
from the Court to the forest. She falls to her knees at the
edge of the clearing*) I can still hear his hateful words—
(*The* HUSBAND *sits, tied to the bamboo stump—his face tense
and pale, his eyes tightly shut. The bandit is leaning against
a tree, gulping wine from a small goatskin. He has evidently
had enough to be boisterous—and dangerous. As he drinks,
some of the wine spills down his bare chest and spatters his
garment. He wipes his mouth with a hairy forearm, taking
a few steps in the direction of the woman*)

TAJOMARU Ey—you! Know who I am? Tajomaru! (*Bellow-
ing, as she doesn't react*) Don't you have ears? I said—
Tajomaru! Where do you come from that you haven't heard
of Tajomaru? (*He glares at her, then lets out a short, hard
laugh*) Well, you've heard of it now. (*He raises the goatskin
pouch to his lips again. It is empty. Annoyed, he tosses it
aside and, leaning against a tree, pulls a peach out from a
fold of his garment*) You can boast about it when you're an
old hag—(*He bites into the fruit noisily*)—that you were
once raped by the famous Tajomaru, the fisherman's son
who owns the forest! (*The mouthful of peach is rotten. He

grimaces and spits it out. Drawing his sword, he severs the rotten part of the peach in his hand, shoves the remainder into his mouth) And don't look so—outraged. In your whole life it may be the only thing you'll ever remember. (*Wiping his sticky hand on his garment, he turns and surveys the* HUSBAND—*nudges him with his foot, disdainfully*) You like swords, eh? With gold handles. And jewels—red, green. Your fat tongue hung out, didn't it? (*Scowling darkly*) Well, Tajomaru always keeps a promise. Here's a sword for you!

    (*He raises his sword as if to kill the* HUSBAND *with one blow*)

WIFE (*Suddenly screaming*) No!
    (*She springs up and runs wildly toward* TAJOMARU. *He turns, directing his sword toward her. She stops as close to him as she dares. Their eyes hold for a moment*)

TAJOMARU Why not? (*With brutish humor*) I'll only do you a favor by killing him.

WIFE (*Full of loathing*) You—animal!
    (*The smile fades from* TAJOMARU's *face. In swift anger, he extends the sword menacingly toward the* WIFE's *heart as she stands facing him. There is a long, dangerous moment. Then, slowly, his arm relaxes, the sword lowering*)

TAJOMARU Yes, I am an animal. (*With the point of his sword,*

35

he lifts the hem of her robe a few inches and lets it fall, contemptuously) A pity you're not.

> *(Then, without warning, he turns and goes off into the forest. For a long moment, the* WIFE *stands there, almost unable to believe it)*

WIFE   He's gone—(*She runs quickly to her husband, dropping to her knees and drawing his sword*) He's gone—and we're still alive! (*Suddenly, she is overcome by hysterical sobs and laughter, and it is with difficulty that she collects herself enough to cut his bonds*) Forgive me—it's only because I'm so grateful—(*She takes one of his hands in hers, raising it tenderly to her cheek*) I watched your hands cutting against the rope till the blood came. How horrible it must have been for you, my husband. But I want you to know—(*Leaning against his shoulder*)—he couldn't hurt me—all his coarseness, all his brutality—because I thought only of our life together. He couldn't touch that. (*Her arms creep about his neck*) I'll forget it, my love. I promise you. And we'll go on as we—(*She stops as her eyes meet his for the first time. Her arms drop slowly from his neck. She stares at him, then backs away*) Why do you look at me like that? (*He doesn't answer or move—just looks at her with cold, silent contempt*) Your eyes—(*Backing farther away*) What is that I see in them? (*Shaking her head in growing horror*) No—you can't mean it! (*Covering her face with her hands*) I won't look! I won't! (*She starts to cry. The* HUSBAND *sits, motionless, unmoved, staring at her. Suddenly she rises, picks up his sword and holds the handle out to him*) Here—take it and kill me! If

Claire Bloom and Noel Willman,
as the WIFE and the HUSBAND

that's how you feel, kill me! (*Anguished*) Kill me! But don't look at me with such—contempt—(*He sits, his expression unchanging, not taking the sword from her hand. Slowly, her arm drops*) Not even that. You are cruel. (*She starts away, then turns to look back at him, helpless, bewildered*) I never knew any man but you—I never wanted one. I didn't ask for this to happen to me—(*As he remains silent*) What do you want me to do? Go away and never see you again? Where would I go? What would I do—without you? (*Suddenly her pride rebels*) Answer me. Am I so low that you can't throw me a word—like a bone to your dog? (*His silence lights the fuse of her temper*) Answer me! (*She moves toward him with rising anger*) I am no longer the daughter of a maidservant in your house. I am your wife! I've shared your table and your bed! Answer me! (*His eyes continue to despise her. She raises the sword above him*) Answer me! (*Hysterically*) *Answer me! Answer me!*

(*The lights black out, and we hear the sound of the* WIFE *sobbing in the darkness. When the lights come up on the Police Court, she is moving dazedly into its light. She sinks to her knees, her body sagging forward emptily. The* MOTHER *looks at her daughter with an understanding and compassion she has never known before. Then—awkwardly, tentatively—she puts out a hand to comfort her. At the touch, the* WIFE's *head falls forward into her* MOTHER's *lap. The* MOTHER *sits for a long moment, her eyes moist, gratefully stroking her daughter's hair. After a moment, she looks up at the* MAGISTRATE *as if in answer to something he has said*)

37

MOTHER What, Your Excellency? . . . Yes—yes, I'll ask her. (*To her daughter, gently*) Kinume, the Court wishes to know if you have anything more to tell.

WIFE (*Raising her head, dully*) What else is there? (*Then, trying*) I must have fainted. When I came to, I found my husband dead, the sword in his breast. (*Lowering her anguished face*) It was then I knew I had killed him. I ran into the woods, deeper and deeper. I tried to drown the sight of myself in the river. But even the river scorned me. (*She looks up at the* MAGISTRATE *in poignant appeal*) I can't be that worthless, can I? (*The lights have slowly dimmed out, leaving only her face in a spotlight*) Can I?

(*Slowly, the spotlight on her face fades out completely*)

Curtain

ACT TWO

ACT TWO

The time is immediately following the end of Act One. As the lights slowly come up on the Rashomon Gate, the rain is still falling. The PRIEST, *the* WOODCUTTER *and the* WIGMAKER *are in the same positions in which they were last seen—the* PRIEST *and the* WOODCUTTER *obviously moved by the recountal of the* WIFE's *story. The* WIGMAKER, *however, is unimpressed.*

WIGMAKER (*Mimicking the last words and tone of the* WIFE) I can't be that worthless, can I? Can I?

PRIEST Her face—it's so hard to forget.

WIGMAKER Aah! (*A gesture of dismissal*) So—her lips trembled, she cried. Tears are always women's weapon against men. And we idiots believe them every time.

PRIEST But why? Why should she confess to a crime she didn't commit?

WIGMAKER Who knows why women do things? Their minds work in devious ways. To win sympathy, maybe. See how your heart bleeds for her? She confesses to a murder, but—

you can't forget her face. It's so pale and tearful and honest. And honesty is such a virtue—how can you think of hanging a virtuous woman?

WOODCUTTER (*To the* PRIEST, *who has turned away*) Don't let him hurt you. He's—he's only baiting you.

PRIEST What does it matter? (*Wearily*) Some of what he says is true. How can we believe the wife's story—since we heard the medium?

WIGMAKER (*Stares at him for a moment*) The medium?

WOODCUTTER (*Nodding*) They brought a medium to the court.

PRIEST To evoke the spirit of the murdered man.

WIGMAKER So the husband spoke from the dead! (*Eagerly*) What did he say? (*He looks at the* PRIEST, *who doesn't answer—then at the* WOODCUTTER, *who looks away*) Was it so different, then, from what the others said?

PRIEST (*Half to himself*) The wife's anguish—how could that be false? (*Shaking his head*) And Tajomaru, so contemptuous of the rope. Why should *he* lie—a man who's condemned to die?

WIGMAKER And yet—if there's little reason for a man to lie when he faces death, how much less when he *is* dead? (*The* PRIEST *drops his head into his hands, tormented. In the dark-*

42

ness a sound fades in—the sound of rattle-like bells being swung in a weird rhythm. Coming up behind the PRIEST, *with malevolent persistence)* The dead man—what did he say? *What did he say?*

(The lights have started to dim down on the Rashomon Gate and to come up on the Police Court. The MEDIUM, *black hair streaming about her face, holds a divining stick with a cluster of rattle-like bells at the end of it, which she swings with wild fervor. Her eyes are closed, her face possessed, her breathing labored—the inducing of the trance is like a fantastic ballet. Swaying, writhing, she struggles to establish contact with the dead man. When she does, the bell drops from her hand and she falls to the floor. The* HUSBAND's SOUL-VOICE, *hollowly sonorous in its passage from the world beyond, is heard as though emanating from the* MEDIUM's *tortured mouth, though the lips merely open and close emptily)*

HUSBAND's SOUL-VOICE I'm in the dark now—in the empty, whirling pit of darkness. Curses upon you! Curses upon you who threw me into this black inferno! *(As the* MEDIUM *lifts her contorted face, the* HUSBAND's *agonized moan seems to come through her lips. She gasps for breath, then finds it, as the* VOICE *continues)* I will tell you—I want you all to know—how it came to be. *(The* MEDIUM *sways in her trance)* The bandit, after attacking my wife, sat beside her—on the dry bamboo leaves—*(The lights have faded to a small spot on the* MEDIUM's *face, and begin to come up on the forest. There, the bound* HUSBAND *sits, his* SOUL-VOICE *still coming*

43

from the direction of the MEDIUM. *The* WIFE *is half sitting, half lying on the ground—her shoulders hunched forward, her loosened hair hanging down over her face, masking her eyes. The bandit sits beside her, talking to her with quiet intensity*) He spoke to her with a serpent's tongue—like a man who knows of women. And every once in a while—he touched her.

(*Tajomaru's hand moves to the woman's hair*)

TAJOMARU (*Huskily*) It shines, your hair, like the river under the summer moon. I sleep there sometimes, when it's hot— the riverbank still warm from the day's sun—so warm your body needs no clothing. And the heavy scent of the night flowers makes your dreams wild, and you wake up, trembling with desire—(*The* WIFE *sits motionless, giving no indication that she hears him*) But what do you know of things like that, locked in a bamboo box in the city, tied to a man of— silk? (*He moves toward the* HUSBAND *contemptuously*) The samurai warrior! The proud blood of his ancestors has thinned to water with too much easy living. Can those fine hands bruise your skin when they hold you? Or that careful mouth—can it conquer yours? (*He snorts, coming back to her*) Such men are made for women who have ice in their loins. (*Moving closer*) But you are not such a woman. That's what I guessed when the breeze blew and I first saw your face—the cool skin denied by those lips, full and promising. And now that I've—tasted them—

(*The* WIFE *raises her head. Face flushed, lips parted, she looks at the bandit*)

HUSBAND'S SOUL-VOICE   My wife—my loving and gentle and dutiful wife—never in all our married life did I see her face like that. Never—never—!

(*With a breathless sigh, she puts her hand against the bandit's bare chest, then her lips—slowly moving them up to meet his mouth. He pulls her into his arms and they embrace feverishly, passionately. The* HUSBAND *closes his eyes against the sight*)

WIFE   (*Breathlessly*)   Take me! Take me away with you! (TAJOMARU *smiles exultantly. He gets to his feet, lifting her up in his arms, and starts to carry her off*) Wait! (*He stops, looking down at her wonderingly. She turns and looks back at the* HUSBAND, *her eyes narrowing*) As long as he lives I'll always be his wife. I can never be completely yours. (*Coldly*) Kill him. (*There is a moment, as* TAJOMARU *just looks at her. Then, slowly, he drops her to her feet. She points toward her* HUSBAND *with mounting violence*) Kill him! Kill him!

HUSBAND'S SOUL-VOICE   Those words still roar around me like a storm, blowing me deeper and deeper into this bottomless pit. Have such cursed, such foul words ever been uttered out of a human mouth? Even the bandit—this wild beast of the forest—even *he* shuddered. (TAJOMARU *stares at the* WIFE *as she turns and moves back toward him*) He looked at her and something happened in his face—some dim stirring, some deep revulsion against the female animal who feeds on her mate.

(*Suddenly* TAJOMARU *grabs her by the throat and throws*

her to the ground. She tries to crawl away, but he stands astride her)

TAJOMARU (*To the* HUSBAND) What do you want me to do with her? Cut her black heart out? Or spare her? (*As the* WIFE *struggles, he puts his foot on her back, stopping her*) Whatever you say—I'll do it—(*The* HUSBAND *turns his face away, moved by the bandit's unexpected sensitivity. Taking his foot off the* WIFE *and coming toward the* HUSBAND) Come, tell me. It's up to you. (*The* WIFE *scrambles to her feet and runs for her life, off into the woods.* TAJOMARU *wheels and starts after her—but he stops abruptly at the edge of the clearing as her screams are heard disappearing through the woods. He turns back*) Let her go. Her screams will bring someone from the road. (*With sudden decision*) The devil take both of you—I'd better look out for myself. (*He starts to go off in the direction opposite the one the* WIFE *took, but stops, looking back at the* HUSBAND. *Quickly, he crosses to him and cuts his bonds*) We're both better off without her.
(*He exits. The* HUSBAND's *arms sink to his sides. He sits there alone, motionless*)

HUSBAND'S SOUL-VOICE It was quiet—for a long time. Then I heard someone sobbing. Someone sobbing—who could it be?
(*The* HUSBAND's *eyes are filled with tears. Suddenly he bends forward, hiding his face, racked with quiet sobbing —a man whose life, whose hopes, whose pride are gone. Rising finally, he moves about blindly, then leans his*

head against a tree, fighting to regain the control which is the rule of his life. When he finally raises his head, his face is again impassive, inscrutable. He draws his sword, looks at it with silent resolution. As he raises it above his breast, the lights on the forest black out. Simultaneously, the lights come up on the Police Court as the MEDIUM *screams convulsively and, with a motion as if thrusting a sword into herself, pitches forward on her face*)

HUSBAND'S SOUL-VOICE   A lump rose to my mouth, but I felt no pain. Only a coldness creeping along my fingers—and a thin mist gathering around me. Everything was silent. Not a single bird note in the sky, not a leaf moving. Only a lonely light lingered in the grove and on the mountain. In the stillness, I lay quietly. By and by the light grew fainter, till the bamboo and cedars were lost to view. Then someone seemed to approach softly. Who? I tried to see—but the darkness was too heavy. Someone—that someone's hand—grasped the sword in my breast and drew it out slowly. The lump in my mouth rose up to end my breath—and I sank down, down into the blackness of space.

WOODCUTTER'S VOICE   (*In the darkness, violently*)   It's a lie! A lie!

(*There is a crash of thunder as the lights change quickly to the Rashomon Gate, revealing the* PRIEST *and the* WIG-MAKER *staring at the* WOODCUTTER, *who has sprung to his feet*)

47

WOODCUTTER His whole story is a lie! He didn't kill himself! He was—(*He stops as he realizes what he is saying*)

WIGMAKER (*Rising*) He was—what? (*As the* WOODCUTTER *turns away, mopping his brow nervously*) Why are you sweating so? (*The* WOODCUTTER *stops mopping abruptly*) Could it be that you have some little morsel you're not sharing with us?

WOODCUTTER No. I—I don't know anything.
(*He meets the* PRIEST'S *searching eyes, avoids them quickly*)

WIGMAKER (*Grinning*) Just that a dead man lied. Only that.
(*The* PRIEST *gets slowly to his feet, his eyes never leaving the* WOODCUTTER)

WOODCUTTER I don't know—maybe he *didn't* lie—
(*He starts away*)

PRIEST (*To the* WOODCUTTER) It is *you* who are lying.

WOODCUTTER (*Stopping and turning back*) I swear—

PRIEST You swear too easily. Now—and in the Court today. (*As the realization unfolds*) But you did not find a *dead* man —you saw him *alive*—and the bandit and the woman—

WIGMAKER (*Delighted*) He must have seen the whole thing!

PRIEST (*Crossing to the* WOODCUTTER) Why? Why didn't you tell them at the Court yesterday?

(*The* WOODCUTTER *meets the* PRIEST's *relentless gaze.
Then, slowly, his shoulders sag, his lips tremble*)

WOODCUTTER   I'm—a poor man—

PRIEST   Is truth a luxury for the rich?

WOODCUTTER   I—I didn't want to get involved.

PRIEST   Involved? But you *are* involved! If not by your con-
science or love of truth, then out of pure selfishness. Every
time justice blunders, it is *you* who cries out for mercy, who
rots in every jail, who hangs on every rope! What kind of
fool are you that could unravel this whole web of dishoner
and deceit, and did not speak out? Whatever their motives,
one of those three—at least *one* of them—was telling the
truth!
   (*There is a low rumble of thunder*)

WOODCUTTER   (*Moving away from him*)   No—
   (*He comes face to face with the* WIGMAKER)

WIGMAKER   No?
   (*The* WOODCUTTER *turns away from him*)

PRIEST   (*Staring at him*)   What do you mean?

WOODCUTTER   (*He turns, pained, reluctant*)   None of their
stories was true. They lied—*all* of them.
   (*The* PRIEST *stands looking at him, stunned. The* WIG-
MAKER *looks from one to the other, then slowly bursts*

into mounting sardonic laughter. The WOODCUTTER
stands, apologetic, miserable)

WIGMAKER   Oh, my poor sides! That's one of the best jokes
that's been played on me since my mother bore me. (*The*
PRIEST *crosses abruptly away from them both*) The way he
sat there all this time with a face as blank as the moon's—

WOODCUTTER   I told you—I—didn't want to get—
(*He breaks off guiltily, glancing toward the* PRIEST)

WIGMAKER   Say it. You didn't want to get involved.

WOODCUTTER   I was wrong.

WIGMAKER   Why? Your first thought was for your own skin—
nothing wrong with that. As for justice, it'll blunder no matter *what* you do. So just trust your own good sense and keep
out of its way.

PRIEST (*Turning*)   Leave him alone!

WIGMAKER   What are you offering him that's any better? Have
you ever rotted in one of those prisons—or felt the cold point
of the policeman's sword at your throat? Yes, courage is an
easy word—in the sanctuary of the Temple garden.

PRIEST   I want no sanctuary!

WIGMAKER   What *do* you want? (*As the* PRIEST *looks at him, at*

50

a loss) You can't even look at the dirty face of the world you live in without wanting to run from it. Or accept the familiar fact that three people told lies in a Police Court yesterday. (*With mock sympathy, as the* PRIEST *turns away*) I know— it's not pleasant, when you're sleeping, to have the pillow kicked from under your head.

PRIEST   There must have been some reason—

WIGMAKER   But it's so simple. Everyone tells what he wants the world to believe.

PRIEST   No. There must be a better answer.

WIGMAKER (*Shaking his head*)   Still hoping for some heavenly hocus-pocus to turn the stink into incense. (*Then*) You were running away, holy man. Well, keep running, I tell you. Don't wait for the miracle.
(*There is a moment, then the* PRIEST *turns and stares at him penetratingly*)

PRIEST   Maybe the miracle is here—now. (*As the* WIGMAKER *looks at him blankly*) Maybe it's you.

WIGMAKER   Me?

PRIEST   The rain—holding us here at the Rashomon Gate. Having to tell again—to you—the whole horrible tale. And out

of your contempt and mockery, uncovering the truth—
(*Looking toward the* WOODCUTTER)—at last.
> (*The* WIGMAKER *follows his gaze to the forlorn figure of
> the* WOODCUTTER, *who doesn't meet their eyes*)

WIGMAKER   At last! The divine mouthpiece! (*He laughs sardonically*) This is your moment, my friend. The hand of Buddha guides your lips!

WOODCUTTER   No, I—

WIGMAKER (*With mock severity*)   Speak up! One doesn't turn his back on Heaven's bidding.
> (*The* WOODCUTTER *looks over at the* PRIEST *helplessly*)

PRIEST (*Gently*)   Never be afraid to speak the truth.
> (*There is a long moment as the* WOODCUTTER *wets his lips.
> Then he nods*)

WOODCUTTER   All right—I'll tell you.

WIGMAKER   Aaah—
> (*He settles himself for the tale*)

WOODCUTTER (*Taking a deep breath*)   I was going through the woods, and—I found this woman's traveling hat—

WIGMAKER   A sedge hat with a veil—we know. And then—?

WOODCUTTER   And then—I heard sounds. So I stole up closer

and peered out from behind a bush. The husband was still alive. He was tied to a tree stump.

WIGMAKER   And the wife?

WOODCUTTER   She was—(*Apologetically*)—fixing her hair.

WIGMAKER   (*Incredulously*)   Fixing her hair? (*To the* PRIEST, *after a moment's reflection*) Of course. What *else* would a woman be doing? (*Turning back to the* WOODCUTTER) And Tajomaru?

WOODCUTTER   He was—on his knees.

WIGMAKER   On his knees? (*As the* WOODCUTTER *nods*) Oh, I'm going to like this story! Tajomaru the Terrible—on his knees!
    (*He laughs, relishing it. As he does, the lights fade out on the Rashomon Gate and come up on the forest, revealing the tableau of* TAJOMARU *kneeling beside the* WIFE, *looking on helplessly as she sits on the ground combing and arranging her mussed hairdo. Her face is averted from him in wordless pique. The* HUSBAND *is bound and gagged at the bamboo stump*)

TAJOMARU   Please—(*He reaches out to touch her, then thinks better of it*) I'm sorry. (*When she just goes on fixing her hair, he moves around on his knees, trying to face her*) How many times can I say it? I'm sorry, I'm sorry. (*She turns her face away from him, leaving him staring at the back of her head again*) Can't you understand? All my life—in here—

(*Taps himself on the temple*)—I've carried around someone like you. When I was a boy, I used to stare at the great ladies passing in their carriage chairs. Once, one of them dropped her fan and I picked it up for her. Her hand was like a toy— with polished nails that curved—like yours—(*He touches her hand reverently. She pulls it away*) Look—I, Tajomaru, known and feared throughout half the country—I'm on my knees, I'm begging you. Please come away with me.

WIFE Leave me alone.
       (*As she continues fixing her hair,* TAJOMARU *springs to his feet, frustratedly*)

TAJOMARU What is it? That I'm a bandit? All right—I give it up. (*As she gives him a disparaging glance, he holds up a hand*) I promise. And I always keep a promise. Ask any beggar or thief and they'll tell you—Tajomaru always keeps a promise.

WIFE (*Disinterested*) Go away.
       (*Getting more desperate,* TAJOMARU *squats down beside her*)

TAJOMARU Is it money? I've got piles of it, hidden away in places all over the forest. Just come with me and I'll show you things to make your mouth water—silks, jade, ivories, jewels! (*She has stopped fixing her hair and is listening*) Remember three years ago when Lord Uji's daughter disappeared on the highway with all her dowry? (*Her head turns slowly*) There's one emerald as big as my fist. (*He holds out his fist—*

she stares at it, eyes wide as saucers, mesmerized) I can just
see how it would look, there, in the hollow of your neck—
(*The "emerald" is moving toward the hollow of her
neck. Almost there, it suddenly becomes a fist again*)

WIFE (*Shrinking away*) Don't touch me!
(TAJOMARU *is bewildered. Then he claps himself on the
forehead*)

TAJOMARU What an idiot! How could I expect a lady like you
to dirty herself with stolen money and jewels. (*He paces
back and forth, the next decision facing him squarely. He
struggles against it—finally submits to the inevitable*) All
right, then, if that's what it has to be, I'll do it. I'll go to work!
(*Kneeling again, eagerly*) Yes, by the dragon's teeth, I'll get
a cart and pull it through the streets. I'll sweat, I'll grow
calluses—but I'll make you happy, if you'll be my woman.
(*The* WIFE *looks at him disdainfully. Rising, she ar-
ranges the folds of her kimono*)

WIFE How can you even *suggest* anything like that?

TAJOMARU How? (*He moves to her on his knees*) Because I
want you so much, I—(*He embraces her, getting to his feet
as she tries to fend him off*) Let me kiss you again—let me
show you!

WIFE (*Struggling against his lips*) No—don't—stop it!
(*Suddenly she gives him an unladylike shove. He stumbles back, his hand which was holding her kimono acci-
dentally ripping it. She stares at the ugly rent, horrified*)

55

WIFE My kimono!

TAJOMARU (*With strained patience*) I'll get you a new one—

WIFE Look what you've done!

TAJOMARU I'll get you *ten* kimonos!

WIFE Only the second time I've worn it—

TAJOMARU (*Bursting*) Hell take your kimono! (*As she looks at him, startled*) Yes, that's what I said—*hell take it!* And hell take *you!* (*Taking a step toward her*) I'll beat you—I'll *kill* you—if you don't do what I say!

WIFE You wouldn't dare! (*Then, hopefully*) Would you? (*He draws his sword menacingly. The* WIFE's *cheeks flush with pleasurable excitement as her eyes survey this forceful, predatory male animal before her. Then, slowly, she draws her fan from her belt. It flutters to her face, her eyes above it —female, provocative for the first time*) What you're asking is unreasonable. How *can* I do what you say?

TAJOMARU Huh?

WIFE A wife's duty is to her husband.

TAJOMARU Oh. (*An idea forms. He crosses to the* HUSBAND) All right, then I'll kill *him*.
        (*He raises his sword as the* HUSBAND *wriggles and gurgles in protest*)

WIFE No—don't!

TAJOMARU (*Turning*) It's the easiest way.

WIFE A lady isn't won by "the easiest way." She only prizes a man who's ready to fight for her.

TAJOMARU (*It had never occurred to him*) Fight? You mean—duel?
> (*Abruptly, the* WIFE *runs to her* HUSBAND *and cuts his bonds with her dagger*)

TAJOMARU Wait—don't! What are you doing? (*Apprehensively*) I don't want to play fancy games with a samurai.

WIFE (*Stepping back, a note of anticipation in her voice*) Now —it's up to *both* of you.
> (*She watches expectantly as her* HUSBAND *removes the rope from around him and the gag from his mouth.* TAJOMARU *takes a defensive grip on his sword handle, backing away warily*)

HUSBAND (*Rising, adjusting and brushing off his robe*) You can put that sword away. (*As the bandit gapes at him*) Don't worry, I'm not going to cut you down.

TAJOMARU Cut *me* down?

HUSBAND I have no intention of engaging in a duel with you.

The sword of a samurai is reserved for nobler causes. It is a weapon of honor.

WIFE   What about—*my* honor?

HUSBAND   You don't even know what the word means.

WIFE   But—I've just been *raped!*

HUSBAND (*A snort of disbelief*)   Ha!

WIFE   I struggled—I was overcome—

HUSBAND (*Scathingly*)   My dear wife, I may have been gagged but I wasn't blindfolded.

WIFE   There was nothing I could do!

HUSBAND   Naturally—being what you are.

WIFE (*The veneer of the "lady" is dropping off fast*)   What do you mean—what I am?

HUSBAND   You just cut my bonds with your dagger. Why didn't you drive it into your throat instead? That's what a woman of true nobility would have done, to wipe out her disgrace.

WIFE   I see. That's what a woman of nobility would have done. But, I, being what I am—

HUSBAND What you are and what you always will be—a kitchen maid's daughter—a slut!
(TAJOMARU *stares at him, aghast*)

WIFE So that's my reward—for all my faithful devotion!

TAJOMARU (*Stunned*) Kitchen maid's daughter?
(*They ignore him completely*)

HUSBAND (*A bitter laugh*) Devotion! Do you think I'm a child? All those smiles at any man who crossed our threshold. You weren't even skillful enough to conceal them behind your fan. And the little sighs in the darkness of our garden— the whispers behind the screens—

WIFE (*Injured*) What whispers?

HUSBAND Oh, you can stop playing the lady now. I'm your husband, remember? I know where you came from and what you are. And I've tried all this time to ignore it and, somehow, to save face.

WIFE (*Shrilly*) Face—face! It's all you ever think about!

HUSBAND I should have thought about it before I married you.

WIFE You boor—you snob!

TAJOMARU (*Suddenly*) Oh, be quiet, both of you! (*They stop and look at him. He surveys them distastefully—viciously*

59

swats a mosquito on his neck) How did all this start, anyway?
(*Remembering, resentfully*) That breeze. I'd still be asleep
by the roadside if not for that stinking breeze. (*Sheathing his
sword*) Let's forget the whole thing.

    (*He starts off, but the* WIFE *runs after him*)

WIFE   Wait—don't go! How can we forget it?

TAJOMARU   I've forgotten it already.

    (*He starts to go again, but the* WIFE *catches his arm*)

WIFE   You can't leave us here like this—you can't!

TAJOMARU (*Disengaging his arm*) Stop following me! I hate
being followed.

HUSBAND   Leave him alone! Haven't you disgraced yourself
enough? (*The two men start away from her in opposite
directions. She looks helplessly from one to the other, then
sinks to the ground, sobbing—her first genuine tears. The
two men stop and turn, then slowly come back and stand
looking down at her*) Oh, stop that whimpering.

TAJOMARU   Women always cry.

HUSBAND   She's just wasting all those tears on *me*. Maybe she
thinks *you* can be fooled by—

TAJOMARU   Me? Not any more.

HUSBAND It was her face that trapped me. I thought I could make something of her, but—

(*He shrugs*)

TAJOMARU Well—you can always put her back in the kitchen.

WIFE (*Springing to her feet*) Kitchen! (*The explosiveness of her action makes the two men take a backward step*) Kitchen maid's daughter! Yes, that's what I am! But one thing you learn in the kitchen is to recognize the smell of—(*At both of them*)—garbage!

HUSBAND Hold your tongue!

WIFE (*Turning on him*) My dear, gallant husband! All that noble talk about your noble sword! Everyone knows a samurai has the right to destroy anyone for the most trifling offense. And what has this man done to you? Overpowered you, bound and gagged you, violated your wife before your very eyes! And your reply to all this? You draw yourself up and order me to drive the dagger into my throat! (*With crushing contempt*) I thought I was giving you one last chance to be a man. But I should have known better. I've lived with you, slept with you, felt you tremble in the night and held your head while you *vomited* before you rode off to battle in glorious splendor. Yes, we both know why you won't fight. You're a coward—(*Shrilly*) Coward—coward—coward!

TAJOMARU (*Repelled by her outburst*) That's enough!

WIFE Enough? (*Turning to him*) Who says enough?

TAJOMARU Tajomaru!

WIFE (*She measures him*) Ah, yes— Tajomaru the Terrible— (*Moving toward him*) For years, I thrilled to the tales of your romantic escapades, your daring, your savage strength. (*Surprised at these words,* TAJOMARU *begins to preen*) And for a moment, I thought it might be true. I half hoped you were the one who would beat me, fight for me, tear me away from this stupid life I've been living. But, no—(*She moves closer to him*) You were ready enough to murder my husband when he was bound and gagged. But when I untied him your burning passion for me vanished—and you can't wait to vanish after it. You're no better than he is—just a small, cheap imitation of yourself, a reputation without a body—a nothing!

> (*She spits full in his face. Slowly, darkly,* TAJOMARU *wipes his cheek. Then, abruptly, he shoves her aside so violently that she crashes back against a tree with an audible gasp. Glaring at her, he slashes the air ferociously with his sword a few times, testing the blade. Then he wheels toward the* HUSBAND. *The* WIFE, *too, turns toward the* HUSBAND. *There is an expectant moment*)

HUSBAND (*It's been rankling all this time*) Vomited, did I! (*Turning toward the bandit, he also tests the blade of his sword, slashing the air with great style. The* WIFE *smiles with triumphant satisfaction as the two men assume en garde positions. For a few moments, the air is filled with shouts and slashes of swords as they swing away with great ferocity—though never coming close enough to touch blades. At last, however, they are forced to approach each other—slowly, cautiously—their extended swords trembling slightly. As they get closer and closer, the* WIFE's *satisfaction changes to apprehension— until, when the tips of their swords finally touch, she lets out a frightened screech, so startling the two tense men that they spring away from each other. Recovering, they glare at her with some annoyance. The two men now circle around each other warily, again going through an elaborate series of feints without coming in actual contact. After a while,* TAJOMARU *stops, a bit winded, and lowers his sword)*

TAJOMARU   Well, why don't you attack?

HUSBAND   Why don't *you?* (TAJOMARU *wipes his nose with his sleeve. Then suddenly he takes a single, mighty leap toward his adversary, swinging a single, mighty blow while roaring out a fierce animal-like sound. It looks very impressive but achieves nothing, since the* HUSBAND *simultaneously takes a mighty leap backward. In retaliation, the* HUSBAND *attacks with a magnificent and highly skilled set of fencing figures. But* TAJOMARU *retreats without the least concern for good swordsmanship or dignity. And they still have not managed to touch each other. The* WIFE, *who has retreated behind a tree, has been peering out at the progress of the "duel." As the bloodless pantomime continues, she emerges slowly from her position of safety. Her* HUSBAND *notices her*) Don't stand in the open like that!

TAJOMARU Get behind a tree! You might get hurt!

WIFE (*Scathingly*) That's more than I can say for either of you!

(*She moves back among the trees as the men look after her sheepishly. Then they turn and spring toward each other with more genuine fury, and this time the forest is filled with the clanging of sword against sword as the character of the duel changes to one of grim reality. Abruptly,* TAJOMARU *swings a wild blow at the* HUSBAND'S *legs. The latter just manages to vault over the whistling sword and aims a return slash at* TAJOMARU, *which misses but cuts through the rope belt holding the lower part of the bandit's kimono tied about his middle.* TAJOMARU *grabs and holds up the kimono with his free hand and continues the duel—but the cloth slips between his legs now and then, tripping him. The* HUSBAND, *sensing his advantage, presses the attack even more vigorously, in and out among the trees and bamboo patches—the bandit defending himself desperately, resorting to every foul trick he knows. And he knows quite a few. Suddenly, while retreating around a tree stump,* TAJOMARU *turns and brings his sword straight down with a vicious grunt, in a blow aimed to split his opponent's skull. But the* HUSBAND *jumps aside and* TAJOMARU'S *sword splits only the air and embeds itself deeply in the tree stump. The bandit tugs frantically but the sword won't come loose*)

HUSBAND (*Triumphantly*) Hah!

TAJOMARU (*Holding up a hand, as the* HUSBAND *advances on him*) Wait—give me a chance—(*But the* HUSBAND *advances relentlessly.* TAJOMARU *backs away*) You can't kill an unarmed man—you can't!
(*As the* HUSBAND *comes toward him, sword held ready for the final thrust,* TAJOMARU *falls backward and tries to grovel away*)

HUSBAND Tajomaru the Great, your time has come!

TAJOMARU (*Green with fear*) No—no—NO!
(*He threshes about, kicking wildly and throwing handfuls of leaves and dirt at the* HUSBAND *to disconcert his aim, all the while whimpering in terror. As a rain of dirt momentarily blinds the* HUSBAND, *the bandit leaps up and clutches his upraised sword arm. In the frenzied grappling that ensues, the sword flies out of the* HUSBAND'S *hand and into a clump of bushes. Desperately, disengaging himself, the* HUSBAND *wheels and disappears into the bushes to retrieve his sword.* TAJOMARU *scrambles back to the stump and tugs again at his embedded sword—but it stubbornly refuses to come loose. He turns in time to see the* HUSBAND *cautiously stealing out from among the bushes, sword in hand. Frantically, he picks up another handful of dirt and throws it at the* HUSBAND, *who stumbles blindly backward into the bushes. There's a chilling cry from the* HUSBAND *as he falls. With a mighty pull,* TAJOMARU *finally frees his sword and turns to de-*

65

fend himself. The WIFE, *who has been following the progress of the encounter from various vantage points, watches with tense expectancy as the bushes slowly part and the* HUSBAND *staggers into momentary view. His sword is impaled deeply in his breast! The* WIFE *gasps*)

HUSBAND   I—I fell—

(*A pathetic look of surprise on his face, he falls backward into the bushes, out of sight. Slowly, the* WIFE *moves over to where she can look down at the body of her* HUSBAND. *Then she turns her eyes toward the bandit. Exhausted, unable to speak, he drops his sword and starts to stagger toward his prize, arms outstretched. But as he does, a wave of revulsion sweeps over her. She backs away from him with a sound of horror and disgust—turns and runs headlong into the forest.* TAJOMARU *tries to follow, but after a few steps he sinks to his knees—stares dumbly off in the direction in which the* WIFE *disappeared. The lights of the forest fade to a dim half-light on the figure of* TAJOMARU *as the lights on the Rashomon Gate come up fully. There, the rain has stopped, but the fire is still burning fitfully. The* WIGMAKER *is listening attentively as the* WOODCUTTER *finishes the story. The* PRIEST, *his head bowed, sits facing away from them both*)

WOODCUTTER   . . . I held my breath, hiding there behind the bush, afraid Tajomaru might hear. But then, when I thought I'd burst, he got up. (*In the forest,* TAJOMARU *gets wearily to his feet*) He picked up his sword. (TAJOMARU *does what the* WOODCUTTER *narrates*) And then—I still get chills when

66

I think of it—he passed by me so close I could have touched him. I didn't move a hair—(TAJOMARU *disappears among the trees. The half-light of the forest fades out completely*)—not until the last echo of his footsteps died away. Then I jumped up and ran as fast as I could—out of the forest—

WIGMAKER   Straight to the Police.

WOODCUTTER   Yes.

WIGMAKER   Only on the way you happened to forget part of the story.

WOODCUTTER   No, I didn't forget. I—(*Rubbing his forehead*) I don't know—maybe I should have spoken up at Court, but —all those different stories—I began to doubt my own senses. I couldn't understand—I still can't understand—why they all lied.

WIGMAKER (*Teasingly*)   Did they?
    (*The sound of the crows is heard again*)

WOODCUTTER   They must have! I know what I saw with my own eyes.

WIGMAKER   Why should I trust *your* eyes any more than those of the other three? Like I told you—people see what they want to see and say what they want to hear. (*As the* WOOD- CUTTER *starts to protest, the* WIGMAKER *holds up a hand, grin- ning*) But don't worry—if I believed any story, it would be yours. Not because of you, but only because it has the smell of truth. It's disappointing, isn't it? You'd like to think people are big—big heroes, big villains, big anything. But no—this is the way they are—small, weak, selfish, cowardly—faithless—(*He looks at the* PRIEST's *back with a smile of triumph*) There's your miracle, holy man.

> (*The* PRIEST's *face is bleak, empty. Picking up his staff and pack, he moves toward the rear of the Gate, stands looking off down the road leading away from the city. The* WOODCUTTER *turns on the* WIGMAKER *angrily*)

WOODCUTTER Why do you keep chopping to bits everything that's good?

WIGMAKER (*Starting to douse the fire*) It's all in the way you look at it. Some people think *trees* are good—yet you chop them down. Me—I have nothing, I am nothing—and I've long since given up deluding myself. To me, truth is a firefly —now you see it, now you don't. And lies—they're no more than the little bugs that go to bed with me. I swat them for amusement—(*With a shrug*) It's the only form of cleanliness I can afford.

> (*There is a sound suddenly, from somewhere in the back —the odd, choked sound of a baby's crying. The three men turn, looking around questioningly*)

WOODCUTTER Listen! That's not a crow! (*The* WIGMAKER *runs off, disappearing behind some large beams*) What is it?

> (*In a moment, the* WIGMAKER *returns, carrying a blanket-wrapped bundle*)

PRIEST (*Dropping his pack and coming over*)   A baby!

WIGMAKER   They're always dumping them here. (*Examining the blanket*) Look at this blanket. Wool—real wool. (*Quickly stripping the blanket off the baby*) It must be worth at least—

PRIEST (*Outraged*)   What are you doing? Give me that child! (*He tears the baby away from the* WIGMAKER, *who manages to hang on to the precious blanket*)

WOODCUTTER   What a vile thing—stripping an infant!

WIGMAKER   Someone's bound to do it. Why not me?

WOODCUTTER   I ought to break your bones.

WIGMAKER (*Moving away*)   Oh, stop being such a hero.

WOODCUTTER   You're just a ghoul—a ghoul!

WIGMAKER (*Turning, stung*)   Then what would you call its parents? They had themselves a little pleasure, then dumped the consequences—like some rubbish. If I'm a ghoul, what are they?

WOODCUTTER   What do *you* know of parents and children?

WIGMAKER (*With a shrug*)   What's there to know? Sometimes they throw you away—sometimes you throw them away.

69

WOODCUTTER Your mind is so twisted! (*Crossing to look at the baby in the* PRIEST's *arms*) Can't you see this isn't a newborn infant? It must be four or five months old. What agonies these people must have suffered—to abandon such a child!

WIGMAKER (*Pained*) Please—I've heard enough sad stories for one day.
(*The baby begins to whimper again*)

PRIEST It's shivering—

WOODCUTTER It'll die of cold. (*Advancing on the* WIGMAKER) Give me back that blanket! (*As the* WIGMAKER *ignores him, folding the blanket deliberately*) Give it back, I tell you!

WIGMAKER (*Dismissingly*) Oh, go away—
(*The* WOODCUTTER *tries to snatch the blanket away from him. They grapple for it—falling to the floor—struggling for its possession. The* PRIEST *takes a step toward them helplessly. With the child in his arms, there is nothing he can do*)

WOODCUTTER (*As they scuffle*) Let go of it!

WIGMAKER Get away!

WOODCUTTER Let go—or I'll—I'll call the Police!

WIGMAKER Call them! Go ahead and call them! (*Struggling to disengage himself*) There are—other things—they might

70

like to know. About—*you.* (*The* woodcutter *stops fighting and stares at him*) That's right—you! (*Scrambling to his feet, still clutching the blanket*) You'd *better* leave me alone. I've been very generous to you—so far.

woodcutter (*Uncertainly*) Generous?

wigmaker Very generous, my friend—my good, honest, self-righteous friend—(*Contemptuously*)—considering that you're a lying hypocrite like all the rest of them! (*Backing off, as the* woodcutter *springs to his feet*) You may have fooled the Magistrate—but not me!
(*The* woodcutter *stops in his tracks, his face going pale. The* priest *looks from one to the other in bewilderment*)

priest What are you talking about?

wigmaker He knows well enough. Ask him—just ask him! (*The* priest *looks at the* woodcutter, *who doesn't meet his eyes. The* wigmaker *speaks pointedly to the* woodcutter) Where is the husband's sword, that fancy sword with the silver handle? Tell me that. No one took it from the scene of the murder—yet the Police couldn't find it. What happened? Did it melt away? Was it swallowed up into the earth?

woodcutter I—don't know.

wigmaker You don't know! (*To the* priest) Just look at his face. (*To the* woodcutter, *relentlessly*) What was it the

Medium said? "Someone approached softly—drew the sword out of the dead man's breast—even before he was cold—"

WOODCUTTER (*Desperately, shaking his head*)   No!

WIGMAKER (*Cocky now, he pokes the* WOODCUTTER *in the chest with a bony finger*)   How much did you get for it? Plenty, I'll bet. And you call *me* a ghoul! (*The* WOODCUTTER *turns to meet the anguished, questioning eyes of the* PRIEST. *Suddenly, he wilts, his head dropping down against his chest*) You were so eager to spare his feelings, I thought I'd help you cover up. You know, as one thief to another. But that's what you get when you try to do someone a good turn. (*The* PRIEST *has turned away, brokenly. The* WIGMAKER *moves to the rear of the Gate, looks off*) Looks like a break in the storm. (*He turns back. The* WOODCUTTER *is slumped against a pillar*) Oh, don't take it so hard. (*Friendlier now*) I once saw a painting—a man hanging by a rope over a precipice. On top were wild beasts ready to devour him if he went up. Down below lay a dragon waiting to catch him if he fell. And all the time a white rat, representing day, and a black rat, representing night, were gnawing away at the rope. (*Patting him on the shoulder, encouragingly*) That's the way it is, my friend. So let's not argue about right and wrong, the few minutes we're dangling here. (*He moves toward the rear of the Gate again, turns*) Anyway, my thanks to you—both—for such an entertaining afternoon. (*Holding up the blanket*) And profitable, too.

(*He laughs, tucking the folded blanket into his shirt as he hurries away through the rear of the Gate and out of sight. For a long while, the two men stand silently, not looking at each other. Then the* PRIEST *crosses to get his pack. As he bends to pick it up, the baby begins to cry again. He straightens quickly, shifting the baby in his arms. The* WOODCUTTER *has raised his head and is watching as the* PRIEST *tries inexpertly to comfort the infant with awkward pats)*

WOODCUTTER (*Coming over, hesitantly*) Please—(*Holding out his arms*) Let me—

PRIEST (*Turning away, harshly*) Let you what? Strip off the rest of its clothes?
(*The* WOODCUTTER *draws back, his lips trembling*)

WOODCUTTER I know. And I don't blame you. Why should you trust me? But—(*As always, the words come hard*) I have six of my own at home. Hungry, sometimes—cold, frightened. They cry, too. (*The* PRIEST *turns back slowly, beginning to take in the meaning behind the words. Under his gaze, the* WOODCUTTER *lowers his eyes apologetically*) What can I say? (*A helpless gesture*) A silver-handled sword can dry a lot of tears.
(*The baby's crying becomes more violent, choked. The* WOODCUTTER *finds it impossible to do nothing. Tentatively, he reaches out his arms toward the child again*)

WOODCUTTER Please—(*This time the* PRIEST *makes no move to stop him as he takes the baby. Expertly, yet tenderly, he puts it over his shoulder, patting and rubbing its back as he makes*

73

comforting little sounds. The baby's crying trickles off and stops. The WOODCUTTER *looks over at the* PRIEST *reassuringly*) Gas. (*He removes the baby from his shoulder and cradles it in his arms*) It will be hard for you to travel—with an infant. The road is often steep—lonely—(*Hesitantly*) Maybe—I could take it home with me. There's little enough, but—(*Looking down at the baby, he smiles*) How much can such a small mouth eat? (*The* PRIEST *stands looking at him, wordless suddenly in the midst of an immense, dawning comprehension. At his silence, the* WOODCUTTER *holds out the child*) I'm sorry—I shouldn't have asked.

PRIEST   No—keep it. (*As the* WOODCUTTER *stares at him*) Take it with you.

WOODCUTTER   But—you heard it yourself—I'm a coward, a thief, a liar—

PRIEST (*Nodding*)   You're many things. A man—like all men. (*The* WOODCUTTER's *eyes slowly fill with tears*)

WOODCUTTER   Then you—forgive me?

PRIEST   Forgive you? (*Looking off toward the city*) I'm the one who must go back to be forgiven. I thought only of how much I could teach the people. (*He looks at the* WOODCUTTER) But it is you who teach me.

WOODCUTTER (*Shaking his head dumbly*)   I'm afraid I—I'm still too ignorant to understand.

PRIEST (*With a half-smile*) I thank Buddha for such igno-rance.

(*He bows respectfully. Embarrassed, the* WOODCUTTER *bows back*)

WOODCUTTER (*Peering off*) The rain has stopped. (*As the* PRIEST *goes to pick up his staff and pack*) The sun will soon dry the ground, the trees—(*Looking around him*)—the Gate.

PRIEST (*Following the* WOODCUTTER'S *eyes*) The Rashomon. Somehow, it's no longer so fearsome—with all its crows and corpses and jackals. (*Looking down at the baby*) Even out of its crumbling ruins can come—life. (*The Temple bells sound the hour. As the* WOODCUTTER *looks off, the* PRIEST *understands*) It's late. They'll be looking for you at home.

WOODCUTTER I'd better go.

(*The* PRIEST *smiles at him. The* WOODCUTTER *smiles back—then goes down the steps of the Gate. There he turns to look back at the* PRIEST)

PRIEST And thank you.

(*At a loss for words, the* WOODCUTTER *bows. The* PRIEST *returns the bow even more deeply. Shifting the baby in his arms, the* WOODCUTTER *turns and hurries away, dis-appearing into the forest. The* PRIEST *stands looking after the* WOODCUTTER *until he is out of sight. Then he turns, his face at peace for the first time since we've seen him. He glances off at the road he was heading for—moves to the head of the steps. The air is clean and sweet after*

75

the rain. He takes a deep breath, hoists his pack over his shoulder—then starts back toward the Temple bells, toward the teeming city and his unfinished work)

Curtain